Explore Your Senses

SIGHT

by Laurence Pringle

BENCHMARK BOOKS

MARSHALL CAVENDISH
NEW YORK

The author wishes to thank Dr. Edward J. Kormondy, Chancellor and
Professor of Biology (retired), University of Hawaii-Hilo/West Oahu for
his careful reading of this text and his thoughtful and useful comments.
The text has been improved by Dr. Kormondy's notes, however the
author assumes full responsibility for the substance of the work,
including any errors that may appear.

Benchmark Books
Marshall Cavendish Corporation
99 White Plains Road
Tarrytown, NY 10591

Library of Congress Cataloging-in-Publication Data
Pringle, Laurence P.
Sight / by Laurence Pringle.
p.   cm. — (Explore your senses)
Included bibliographical references and index.
Summary: Describes the the parts of the eye and how they work and discusses
such topics as color blindness, visual perception, eye care, and more.
ISBN 0-7614-0734-0
1. Vision—Juvenile literature. [1. Vision. 2. Eye. 3. Senses and sensation.]
I. Title. II. Series: Pringle, Laurence P.   Explore your senses.
QP475.7.P75   1999   612.8'4—dc21   98-28040   CIP   AC

Printed in Hong Kong

6   5   4   3   2   1

Photo research by Linda Sykes Picture Research, Hilton Head, SC

Cover photo: FPG International / David Waldorf
Picture credits: The photographs in this book are used by permission and through the
courtesy of: Photo Edit: 5 (right), David Young-Wolff. Photo Researchers: 6 (left) Hart Davis/
Science Photo Library; 6 (right) Hart Davis/Science Photo Library; 16 (top) Leonard Lessin;
16 (bottom) Leonard Lessin; 17; 18 Vanessa Vick; 20 (bottom) Rod Planck; 21 Rod Planck;
22 (bottom); 23 (bottom); 23 (top) Stephen Parker; 29 (left) Richard Nowitz. Stock
Boston: 20 (top) Michael Dwyer. The Image Bank: 4 (bottom) Patti Mc Conville; 5 (top)
Paul Simcock; 22 (top) James Carmichael; 25 (top) Joseph Drivas; 25 (bottom left) Derek
Berwin; 25 (bottom right) Derek Berwin; 29 (bottom right) Schmid-Langsfield.

Contents

Look around. What do you see? Most people see plenty. With their sense of sight, humans can see many colors, and objects near and far. They can instantly identify all sorts of things, including the faces of friends and family members.

We see three dimensions, not flat pictures. This helps us judge the size of faraway objects. We can also judge the distance and speed of moving objects. This helps us catch a football or kick a soccer ball.

Of all our senses, sight may be the most important. Of all the information taken in by our senses, an estimated 80 percent comes in through our eyes. Every second you are awake, your eyes gather information and send it to your brain. That is where seeing actually occurs. Your eyes and brain are a team. They are always busy, whether you are dancing, dribbling a basketball, playing a computer game, or simply reading these words.

Humans have much better vision than most animals. However, some creatures see colors that are invisible to us. Other animals can see in the dark more clearly than we can. The sense of sight helps different kinds of animals get food and avoid danger. It helps people do these things, too—and much, much more.

Your Sense of Sight

We see so much—colors, motions, objects near and far—
as the sense of sight helps us work and play every day.

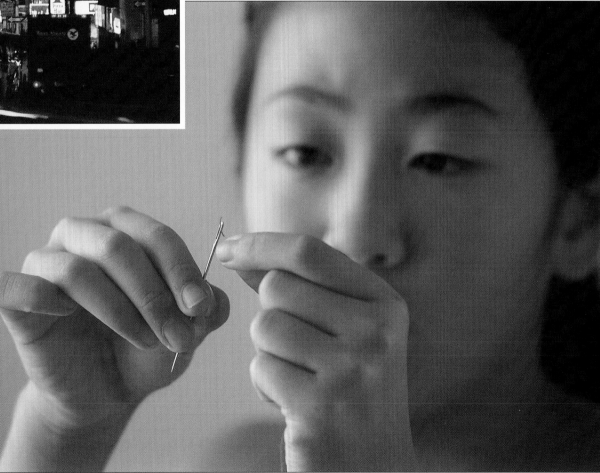

The snowball fight is fun—until you see a snowball hurtling toward your face! It's too late to duck, but your eyelids snap shut. The snowball hits the skin of an eyelid, not the outer surface of your eye.

Vision is precious, and human eyes are protected from harm in several ways. In addition to your eyelids closing instantly when something harmful comes near, they automatically close and open thousands of times every day. These blinks sweep a fresh wash of fluid we call tears over the outer surface of your eye.

Tears flow from glands (called *lachrymal glands*) located just above each eye. Tears are mostly water, but they contain a chemical called *lysozyme* that helps kill germs. So tears help protect eyes from infection. This fluid also keeps the outer eye surface moist and washes away little dust particles. If the wind blows sand or grit onto the surface of your eye, your eyelids automatically blink more and more, bringing more tears to wash the objects away.

Each blink sweeps fresh tears over the surface of the *sclera*. This tough white layer covers almost all of your eye, but normally we see only a small part of it. We call the sclera the "white" of the eye.

Right in the center of the "white" of the eye, is the transparent *cornea*. All of the sclera, including the cornea, is tough and is another protector of the eye. But the cornea has other vital jobs: It is a round

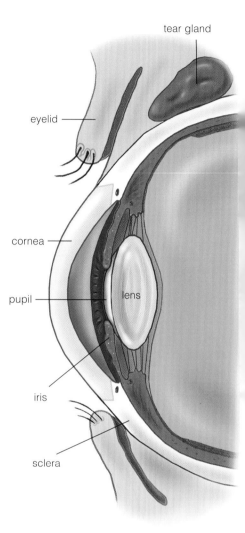

tear gland

eyelid

cornea

pupil

lens

iris

sclera

window through which light passes into the inner part of your eye. It also acts as a lens, helping to focus the light deep in your eye.

Just behind the cornea lies the round *iris*. This is the part of your eyes that people refer to when they say you have blue or brown or another color eyes. Irises can also be colored gray, green, or hazel. A substance called *melanin* gives irises their color. Melanin also helps keep too much light from harming the inner eye.

If we call the cornea a window, then the iris is a shade or a drape. It moves to allow more or less light into the eye. The iris always has an opening in its center, called the *pupil*, through which light passes. However, the size of the pupil changes. In very dim light, the muscles of the iris relax, opening the hole as wide as possible to let light inside your eye. In very bright light, muscles of the iris contract, closing the pupil down to a little dot. This protects the inside of the eye from harm.

The size of your pupil also changes with your feelings. It grows larger when you concentrate on something, or are afraid or excited. In fact, when two people begin to fall in love, the pupils of their eyes usually widen when they meet!

The size of your pupils change with light, and sometimes with feelings.

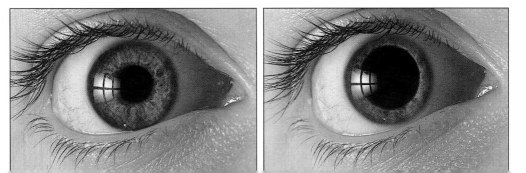

When you look in a mirror, you see only a small part of your eyes. Beneath your skin, set in sockets so they are protected by your bony skull, are two round eyeballs. Each is about the size of a table-tennis (ping-pong) ball.

Without moving your head, you can move your eyeballs—up, down, right, left. Your eyes can also move slightly outward and inward. You can look quickly in all these directions because of six muscles attached to the sclera ("white") of each eyeball.

An eyeball has no bones in it, but needs something to maintain its round shape. Two kinds of liquids do this job. In a small area just behind the cornea the liquid is called the *aqueous humor*. In the large center of the eyeball the jelly-like substance is called the *vitreous humor*. Both humors are clear, so light passes easily through them. When you look in a mirror at the color of your irises, there is aqueous humor in front of them but you cannot see it.

When light passes through the cornea and through the pupil it next passes through the eye's *lens*. It lies just behind your pupil. The lens is made of layers of cells, like the layers that you see when you peel an onion. The lens, however, is not hard like an onion. It looks like a capsule filled with jelly, and is about the size of a pea.

Though the lens is small, it is vital for seeing. Both the lens and the cornea help focus the light that enters the eye. The curved cornea does not change shape, but the lens does. Muscles attached to the lens can change its shape to focus on objects nearby or far away. When you look at something close, the muscles tighten up. This causes the lens to bulge outward. When you look at something far away, the muscles relax and the lens becomes more thin and flat.

After light passes through the lens, it travels through the vitreous humor, then strikes the inner wall of the eyeball. Much of the inner wall is lined with light-sensitive receptor cells. These layers of nerve cells make up most of the *retina*.

If you had eyes only with their pupils, lenses, retinas, and other parts, you could not see. However, the retina makes vision possible by changing light into nerve impulses. These "messages" about the light focused on the retina are carried through the *optic nerve* to your brain. It is there, toward the back of your head, where seeing occurs, as your brain changes nerve messages into the many sights that lie before your eyes.

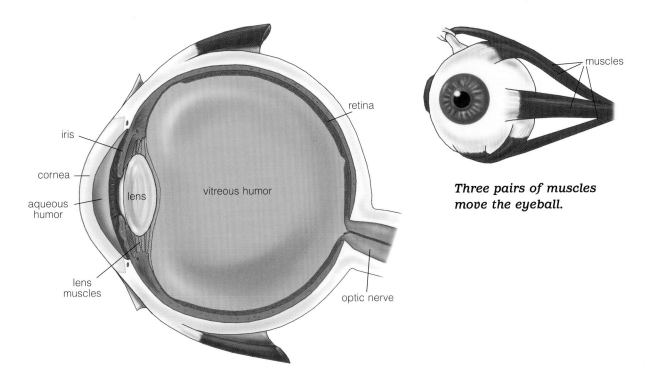

Three pairs of muscles move the eyeball.

People often say that the human eye is like a camera. An eye and a camera are alike in some ways—and dramatically different in others.

In your eye, the lens and cornea focus light on a light-sensitive surface called the retina. In a camera, one or more lenses focus light on a light-sensitive surface called film.

In your eye, the iris opens or closes to adjust the amount of light that reaches the retina. In a camera, a circular shutter can be adjusted to control the amount of light that reaches the film.

In your eye, the shape of the lens is changed by muscles to help make sharply focused images on the retina. In a camera, the lens (or lenses) can be moved forward or back to make clearly focused pictures on film.

In your eye, the light that enters is focused on the retina as an upside down and backward image. Your brain corrects this image so it looks right to you. In a camera, the light that enters is also focused upside down and backward on film. This is corrected when pictures are made from the film.

In these ways your eye and a camera are similar. However, the human eye is much more complicated, and can do much more, than a camera. As you look around, the images on your retina change constantly. In an instant, you can see miles away, then inches away. Everything is seen in three dimensions—as

Better Than a Camera

solid, not flat, objects. Even a camera teamed with
the most powerful computer on Earth is no match
for the team of your eyes and brain.

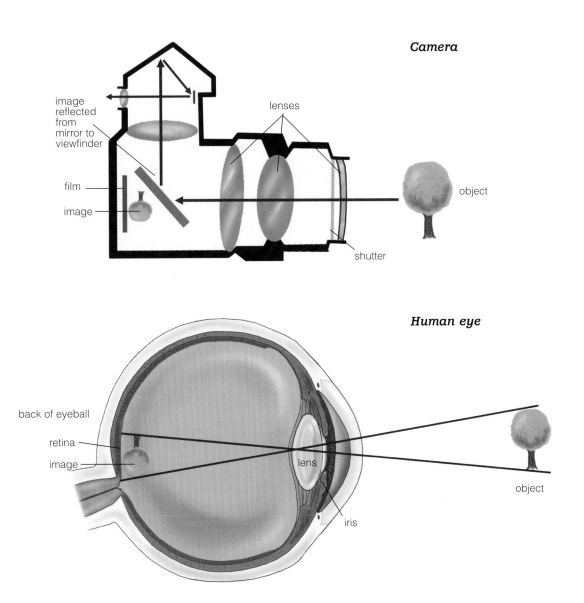

Camera

image reflected from mirror to viewfinder

lenses

film

image

object

shutter

Human eye

back of eyeball

retina

image

lens

iris

object

Very early in your life, when you were developing in your mother's womb, your retinas were part of your brain. As you developed, they became part of your eyes, which are close to your brain and connected to it by optic nerves. Experts on vision still consider retinas to be an outgrowth of the brain.

The retina covers the inner wall of the back half of your eyeball. It is only a hundredth of an inch (a quarter of a millimeter) thick—about as thick as a page in this book. The retina is made up of several layers of cells.

Some of these cells form a network that passes along messages about the light that enters the eye. The messages come from two kinds of light-sensitive receptor cells—*rods* and *cones*— that lie toward the back of the retina. There are about 125 million rods and 6 million cones in each retina.

Cones provide vision in good light. Cone cells also enable you to see colors. In fact, three different kinds of cones exist so you can see all colors. Most cones are concentrated in the center of the retina, in a small yellowish spot called the *macula*. In its center is a little pit called the *fovea*. When you look directly at something or someone, the light is focused on the macula and especially on the fovea. This is where your vision is best. The fovea's tightly packed cones enable you to see fast motions and fine details, all in color.

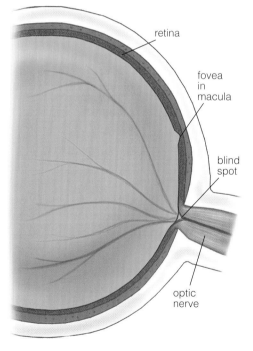

retina

fovea in macula

blind spot

optic nerve

The Amazing Retina

Away from the fovea, the retina has scattered cones and many, many rod cells. Rods enable you to see in dim light. They are about a hundred times more sensitive to light than cones. When you look around at night, in a darkened theater, or in your own room with the lights out, rod cells enable you to see—in black and white and shades of gray, not in color.

As long as there is *some* light—whether sunlight or starlight—your retinas enable you to see. In each eye, about a million nerve fibers carry messages from the retina through the optic nerve to the brain. The place where the optic nerve leaves the eye is called the *blind spot* because there are no rods or cones in that area. However, one of your eyes sees what the other one misses so you do not usually notice the little blind spot in each retina.

●   X

Use your blind spot to make the circle disappear. Hold the book at arm's length. Close your right eye and focus on the X with your left eye. You will still see the circle out of the corner of your eye. Slowly move the page closer to your eyes. The circle disappears when its image is focused on your blind spot.

Even when you stare at something, your eyes move a little and keep scanning the scene in front of them. The images focused on your retina change constantly, and information about the images is sent in a steady stream through the optic nerves.

Nerve fibers cross in a part of the brain called the *optic chiasma*. Messages from the right side of both retinas go to the right side of the brain. Information from the left side of both retinas go to the left side of the brain. Farther back in the brain the nerve fibers enter a kind of switching station, then fan out to different parts of the rear of your brain, including the *visual cortex*.

Scientists are still trying to figure out how the brain enables us to see. They know that several parts of the rear of the brain are involved in making sense of the information from your eyes. If you look at a bird, one part of your brain provides its colors, another its form, a third its motion, and so on. Your brain makes sense of the light collected by your eyes. As long as your eyes are open, it does this continuously.

Even with your eyes closed, your brain provides some vision. You may have heard people say, "I can picture it in my mind's eye." You can do this too. With your eyes closed you can picture people's faces. You can also bring up memories of past events, and create imaginary scenes of the future. While you sleep your brain supplies the vivid images

Seeing With Your Brain

of your dreams, and of nightmares too.

When people who could once see lose their sense of sight, they can still remember what things looked like. Such blind people continue to see, in their mind's eye.

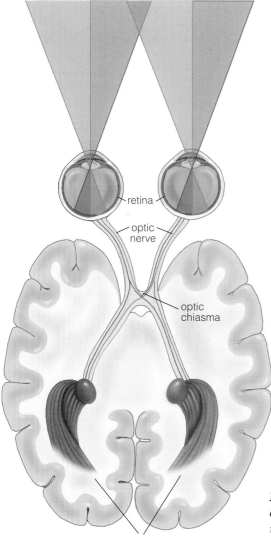

retina

optic nerve

optic chiasma

visual cortex

Images that enter our eyes are actually seen at the rear of the brain, in the visual cortex.

The three different kinds of cone cells in your retinas respond to a range of colors but are especially sensitive to certain kinds of light. One is best at detecting red. A second responds best to green, and the third to blue. Messages from these cone cells are blended in your brain so you can see other colors too. People can identify more than two hundred colors.

The colors of light we see are part of a wider range that is invisible to humans. Beyond violet, for example, is ultraviolet light. People cannot see it because the lenses of their eyes are slightly yellow, and this blocks ultraviolet rays from reaching their retinas.

Ultraviolet can be seen by many kinds of animals, including rodents, birds, fish, amphibians, and insects. Being able to see ultraviolet light is important for honeybees and other insects that get nectar or pollen from flowers. Some flowers that appear as a solid color to humans are actually marked with ultraviolet patterns. The markings attract and guide insects to the food they seek.

We can never know exactly what an insect or bird sees, but scientists have found ways to learn about animal vision. One way is simply to look at whether the animal itself is colorful. Among birds, most males are more brightly colored than females. Color is important when the males court females. Some birds and other kinds of animals eat berries and fruit. They

The top photo shows a flower as humans see it. The bottom photo shows the same flower as it might appear to insects, which see ultraviolet light.

Male birds, like the mallard duck on the right, are usually more colorful than females. Color vision is important in bird courtship.

need to tell whether these foods are ripe. Since color is a clue to ripeness, the fruit-eating creatures probably see in color.

I n dim light, the cone cells in your retinas do not receive enough light to detect colors. You are color blind—but only until the light is bright enough for your cone cells to work. Some people, however, are truly color blind, although "color deficient" is a more accurate term. They do not see all colors well, because of problems with some cone cells or with nerves connecting the retina to the brain.

A few people see only black, white, or grays. This total color blindness is very rare. More common is a problem of telling red and green apart. About eight out of every hundred males have this kind of color blindness. Only one out of a hundred females does.

Color blindness can be detected by showing people special pictures made of small colored circles. In each picture, circles of certain colors form a number or object. People with normal vision can see it. People who are color blind cannot.

Being color blind is not a serious handicap. People learn to identify colors by their shade or tone. They also use other clues. They learn, for example, that the red light of a traffic light is usually on top and the green light is on the bottom. The brightness of these lights shows which one is lit.

Most people see color very well. So do apes, other primates, and ground squirrels. Most other mammals, including mice, rabbits, cats, and dogs, see little or no color.

Some people see only yellow and blue accurately. To them the red light of a traffic signal looks yellow, the yellow light looks like a darker yellow, and the green light looks white.

Color Blind

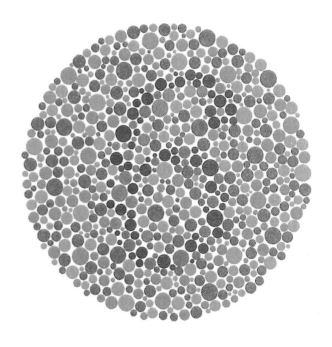

Dot pictures like these are used to test color vision. People with normal color vision see that some dots form a number. People with a color vision defect usually see no number.

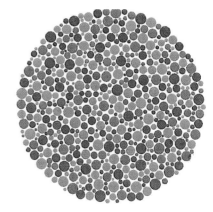

Seeing well in depth—in three dimensions—is important, and we use several clues to judge depth. One is just knowing the size of an object, like a car. If the car looks tiny to us, we know it is far away. Another clue is how parallel lines draw closer together as they go off in the distance. You can see this along a road, railroad tracks, or rows of houses.

Clues like these help you see well in depth, but so do your two eyes working together. If you try shooting a basketball or hitting a tennis ball with one eye closed, you probably won't play well.

As you look at any scene, each of your eyes receives slightly different images. The difference is tiny when you look at something far away because both eyes are aimed straight ahead. When you look at something nearby, however, each of your eyeballs turns inward in order to keep the light focused on the fovea of your retinas. This causes each eye to have a different view.

You can discover this by closing one eye and opening the other, back and forth, a few times. Compare what you see with each eye. You will probably notice that objects in the foreground seem to shift position. They don't, of course, and when you look with both eyes open you see one scene that is a blend of the images from your two eyes.

Seeing in depth with two eyes is called *stereoscopic* vision. It is important for such animals as hawks, cats,

Parallel lines merge in the distance.

Two Eyes Are Better Than One

and other animals that chase quick prey. Seeing well in depth is also vital for monkeys and squirrels that leap from branch to branch in trees. All of these creatures, as well as people, have two eyes in the front of their faces.

Rabbits, deer, and most birds have eyes on the sides of their heads. The right eye takes in images from the right side; the left eye does the same on the other side. These animals can almost see behind their heads! This protects them from enemies, but there is very little overlap between the images from their eyes. They do not have good stereoscopic vision.

Many animals, including the snowshoe hare (left) and the robin (below) see well to the sides but do not have good stereoscopic vision. People once thought that robins tilted their heads to one side to listen for earthworms. Now we know that they look for worms by focusing one eye on the ground.

Your two eyes give you wonderful vision, but most spiders have eight eyes. Do they see even better than you?

Actually, they don't see nearly as well. Compared with humans, spiders have a very simple vision system. Most of their eyes just detect motion. This is just what most kinds of spiders need as they wait for an insect or other prey to come along. Their biggest eyes see in more detail, enabling spiders to identify their prey and catch it.

Many other small creatures also have eyes that do not see shapes clearly but detect motion well. This helps them flee when an enemy approaches. When a sea scallop opens its shell, it peers into the water with a hundred blue eyes. The scallop snaps shut when it detects the slightest movement.

Many insects have two kinds of eyes. The most simple are called *ocelli* (just one is called an ocellus). They are usually located between the larger *compound eyes* of insects. Though simple in structure, ocelli detect the direction of light from the sky and this information helps ants find their way home. In flying insects, ocelli also keep track of the horizon. This helps the insects fly upright.

An ocellus has one lens, like your eye, but compound eyes are made of many six-sided lenses. Each lens is connected to its own nerve cells. Each takes in a bit of the insect's surroundings. No one knows

This spider has eight eyes. Four face front, two look overhead, and one looks to each side.

Animal Eyes

exactly what kind of picture an insect sees with its compound eyes. The more lenses it has, the sharper its eyesight. Some dragonflies have compound eyes made of 28,000 lenses. They catch mosquitoes and other insects on the wing.

Hawks, eagles, owls, and other birds of prey have the sharpest vision of any animal. Owls have very large pupils that let in light on the darkest of nights. Hawks and other daytime birds of prey have many more cone cells packed into the fovea of their retinas than do humans. High in the sky, their keen vision enables these birds to see rabbits and even tiny mice on the ground.

The green darner dragonfly has compound eyes made up of many thousands of simple lenses.

A scallop's blue eyes detect motion and help protect it from enemies. The big eyes of the caterpillar (left) are not real. It sees with small eyes. The false eyes may scare away enemies, allowing the caterpillar to develop into a spicebush swallowtail butterfly.

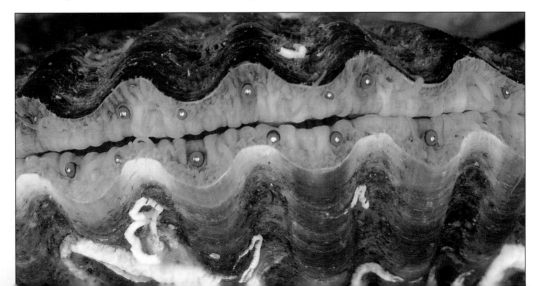

Though some animals can see better than we do, and even see color that is invisible to us, humans have invented ways to extend vision beyond its normal limits. With telescopes, microscopes, and other devices, we see sights no animal can see.

When you look through binoculars or a telescope, their lenses make something far away look close. Since 1609 telescopes have been used to study planets and stars. Modern telescopes use huge lenses or mirrors for this research. These telescopes are usually built on tall mountains so the view into space is not dimmed much by dust and gases in the atmosphere. This problem disappears completely when a telescope is sent beyond the atmosphere, into orbit around the Earth. Space telescopes can send radio signals to Earth that are used to make clear pictures of objects in space.

You may have looked through a magnifying glass or a microscope to get a closeup look at part of a fly or other insect. A magnifying lens can make the fly look as much as eight times bigger than normal. A microscope with two or three lenses can enlarge an object a hundred or even a thousand times. Another kind of microscope enlarges objects even further. The scanning electron microscope uses beams of electrons to produce finely detailed pictures of tiny objects.

Another special device—an *X-ray* machine—may be aimed at your jaw when you visit your dentist. X-rays are invisible to your eyes but they can be recorded on film. They pass easily through muscles and soft parts of your body but are mostly stopped by teeth and bones. So X-ray films allow dentists to check the health of your teeth, and doctors to look for broken bones.

A thin beam of X-rays is used in an instrument called a CAT

Extending Our Vision

scanner. The word CAT stands for *c*omputerized *a*xial *t*omography. This device produces a cross-section picture on a television screen of a person's body or head. CAT scans are especially useful in treating injuries to the brain.

Pictures that help people can also be produced by devices using radio waves. When these invisible waves are sent out they reflect off objects. A reflected wave is called an echo. Received by *radar* equipment, the echoes are used to make pictures on a screen. Radar—which stands for "*ra*dio *d*etection *a*nd *r*anging"—is used to help airplanes fly and land safely. It also helps weather forecasters track storms.

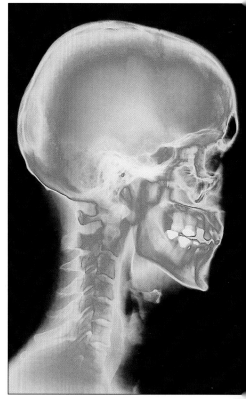

A colored X-ray of a person's head and neck.

Electron microscope views of an ant and a wasp.

There's an old saying: "Seeing is believing." In other words, you can trust what you see. Is this always true? Experts on human vision say that sometimes "seeing is *dis*believing."

Your brain does a remarkable job as it tries to make sense of the constant flow of nerve impulses from your retinas. Every day, however, it has to make countless snap judgments, so it sometimes relies on tricks and shortcuts. Your brain often uses memories of images to fill details not actually seen. It also uses your experience and feelings. Sometimes these factors may cause a person to misjudge reality. What you think you see may not be what is actually there.

Human vision is good at recognizing familiar objects and situations. It is more easily fooled in surprising, unfamiliar situations. When several people witness an auto accident, each one may recall some details differently. In courts, the evidence given by eyewitnesses is not considered very reliable.

Some *optical illusions* on these pages show how your brain can sometimes be fooled. Nevertheless, in everyday life "seeing is believing," most of the time.

Can You Believe What You See?

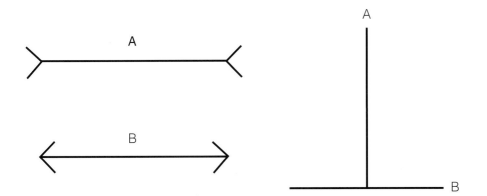

Look at these two sets of lines. Which line is longer, A or B? Just to be sure that your vision can be trusted, measure them.

Are these line parallel? One way to check is to view them from the lower left corner.

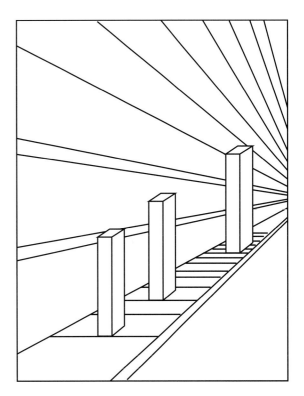

Look at the three blocks, then measure their heights with a ruler.

Everyone should know how to protect his or her eyes from harm. For some jobs, hobbies, or other activities it is wise to wear safety glasses or goggles. Also remember that too much light can damage the cells of your retinas. Never look directly at the sun through a telescope or binoculars. Make sure you eat such foods as carrots and spinach, which contain vitamin A. Rod cells in your retina need this vitamin to give you vision in dim light. Also, rest your eyes after doing a lot of close work or after looking at a computer screen for a long time. Finally, have your vision checked by an eye doctor every two years.

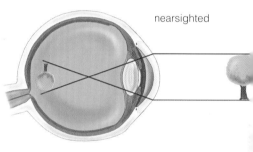

Nearsighted people see close objects well but faraway objects are focused in front of the retina instead of on it.

The sense of sight varies from one person to another. Some people have near-perfect vision all of their lives. Others are born with some difficulty in seeing, or develop a defect later on. One problem called *astigmatism* occurs when the curved surface of the cornea and the retina do not match well. This causes images on the retina to be distorted. When a person with astigmatism looks at an object, one part of it will be clear but another part will be blurry. Sometimes the shape of the eyeball or cornea causes a person to be *nearsighted*. Closeup vision is fine, but distant vision is blurry. The opposite is true when a person is *farsighted*.

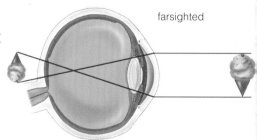

Farsighted people see faraway objects well but close objects are focused behind the retina.

As people grow older their vision usually changes. The lenses in their eyes lose flexibility. As a result,

Taking Care of Your Eyes

older people may have trouble seeing things closeup. They may also develop a *cataract*, a clouding of the lens that causes poor vision. However, most eye defects can be helped by eyeglasses or contact lenses. (Many of these aids to vision are now made of plastic, not glass.)

Operations can also help improve eyesight. Even though there are many mysteries about how vision occurs in the brain, the workings of the eye itself are well understood. Many vision problems can be helped. Take good care of your eyes, and they will continue to let in the colorful, fascinating world that is all around us.

Safety goggles and regular visits to an eye doctor are an important part of guarding your sense of sight.

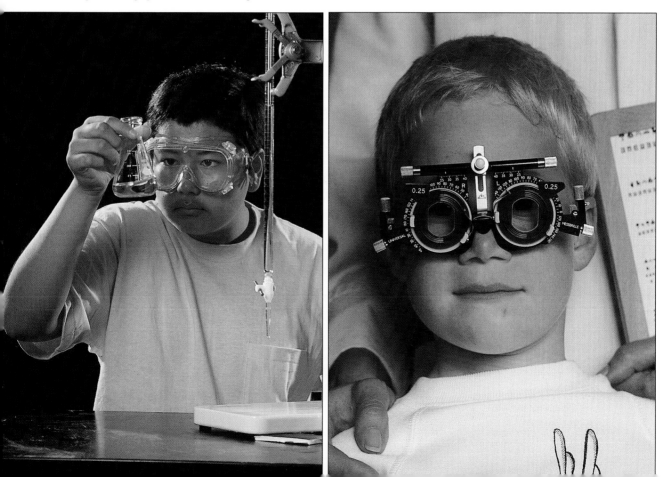

aqueous humor—the clear fluid that fills the chamber between the cornea and the lens.

astigmatism—a vision defect that occurs when the curve of the cornea does not match well with the curved surface of the retina.

blind spot—the small area of the retina where the optic nerve is attached to the eyeball. There are no light-sensitive cones or rods in the blind spot.

cataract—a vision defect caused by clouding of the eye's lens.

CAT scanner—a device that rotates around a person's body or head, allowing thin beams of X-rays to enter the person. A CAT scan picture is produced, which shows a cross-section of the part being scanned. The word CAT stands for *computerized axial tomography.*

compound eye—an eye made up of many small lenses. Insects and crustaceans (including crabs and lobsters) have compound eyes.

cone cells—light-sensitive cells that respond to colors and detect fine details. Cones do not respond in dim light.

cornea—the hard transparent circular area on the front of the eyeball that allows rays of light to enter the eye, and which helps focus the light on the retina.

farsighted—the ability to see faraway things clearly while nearby objects are blurry. It occurs when images of close objects are focused behind the retina, rather than on it.

fovea—the area in the center of the retina where cone cells are most concentrated. It is the part of the retina that produces the eye's clearest, most detailed vision.

iris—the colored part of the eye that surrounds the pupil. The size of the iris changes to allow more or less light through the pupil.

lachrymal gland—a gland just above the eye that produces tears—the fluid that washes the cornea and surrounding sclera and keeps it germ-free.

lens—a small transparent structure behind the pupil of the eye that helps focus light rays on the retina.

lysozyme—a chemical in tears that defends the cornea and surrounding sclera from infections.

macula—a small, yellowish spot in the center of the retina where cone cells are concentrated. They are most abundant in an area of the macula called the fovea.

melanin—dark coloring (pigment) of hair, skin, and the eye's iris. Melanin helps protect the eye from bright sunlight.

nearsighted—the ability to see nearby objects clearly while faraway objects look blurry. It occurs because images of close objects are focused in front of the retina rather than on it.

ocelli—simple eyes with one lens that most insects have on the front of their head. Ocelli help some insects navigate, and flying insects keep track of the horizon.

optical illusion—a picture that can fool the person looking at it, or give a false image of reality.

optic chiasma—the area of the brain where optic nerves from each eye cross to opposite sides of the brain.

optic nerve—the nerve that carries information from the eye's retina into the brain.

pupil—the opening in the iris through which light enters the eye. The size of the pupil depends mostly on the light available, but also on feelings.

radar—a method of detecting distant objects by use of high-frequency radio waves reflected from the objects. Radar stands for *ra*dio *d*etection *a*nd *r*anging.

retina—layers of nerve cells, including cones and rods, that cover the rear half of the eyeball. Light focused on the retina stimulates nerve cells to send information about the light to the brain.

rod cells—nerve cells that are highly sensitive to light. Rods enable us to see in dim light, but only in black, white, and grays, not in color.

sclera—the tough white protective tissue that covers all of the eyeball except for the cornea.

stereoscopic vision—seeing in three dimensions, or in depth, as a result of different images from our two eyes being made into one image in the brain.

visual cortex—the area at the back of the brain that receives information from the eyes. This is where seeing actually occurs.

ultrasound—sound waves of such high frequency that people cannot hear them. Images made from reflected ultrasounds can be used to check the health of an unborn baby in its mother's womb, and can also check the working of an adult's heart.

vitreous humor—the clear jellylike substance that fills the eyeball and supports it from within.

X-rays—invisible radiation that passes through muscles and soft tissues but which is mostly stopped by bones and teeth. X-ray pictures enable us to see within the human body.

Index

Page numbers for illustrations are in boldface.